# WHERE'S WILL?

ILLUSTRATED BY

TILLY

WRITTEN BY

ANNA CLAYBOURNE

**Kane Miller**

A DIVISION OF EDC PUBLISHING

# About
# THIS BOOK

In this book, you can explore ten of William Shakespeare's most exciting, funny, and powerful plays—tales of epic love and romance, adventure and horror, ghosts and witches, silly schemes, magic, grisly murder, and bloody revenge.

For each play, there is a summary to help you understand the story, then you can meet the characters and find out what they get up to. You'll soon see that Shakespeare's stories are packed with high drama, strange goings-on, and weird and wonderful characters.

Then, turn the page and hunt for the characters hidden in a big, detailed picture showing the play's setting. Oh, and don't forget to search for Will himself, too! You'll find him hiding somewhere in each play. And there may even be a cheeky little pig if you look carefully!

William Shakespeare

"All the world's a stage,
And all the men and women merely players;
They have their exits and their entrances,
And one man in his time plays many parts,
His acts being seven ages."

*As You Like It*

# THE PLAYS



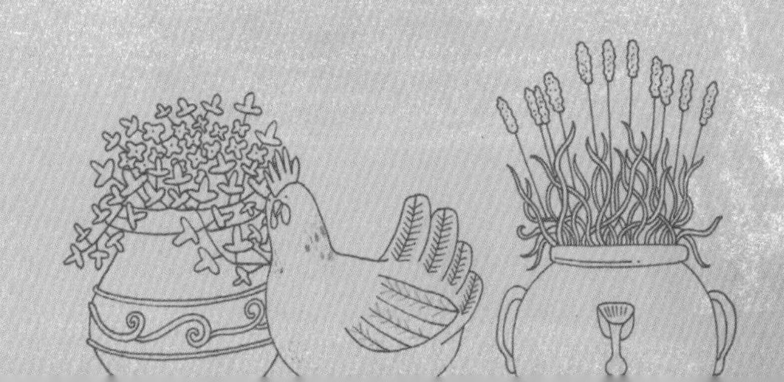

# AS YOU LIKE IT

*Setting: Duke Frederick's court in France and the nearby Forest of Arden*

In this play, you'll find characters dressed up in disguises, including a girl pretending to be a boy. A noblewoman called Rosalind and a young man called Orlando are in love. But when Rosalind disguises herself as a boy, Orlando doesn't recognize her. They have loads of funny conversations with each other, because Rosalind knows who Orlando is, but he doesn't know who she is ... You can imagine how confusing it gets.

A young man named Orlando decides to take part in a wrestling match with a merciless fighter called Charles at Duke Frederick's court. Orlando has no money or education, because his mean older brother Oliver hasn't allowed him to have these things since their father died. Duke Senior should be the duke, but his brother Frederick has taken over. Duke Senior now lives in the Forest of Arden with his followers, but his daughter Rosalind has been allowed to stay at court. She sees Orlando win the wrestling match, and they fall deeply in love. Orlando's old servant Adam warns him that his mean brother Oliver plans to kill him, so he runs away to the forest.

Duke Frederick decides to throw Rosalind out, too. She dresses up as a boy, Ganymede, and sets off for the forest with the jester Touchstone and her cousin Celia (Duke Frederick's daughter), who disguises herself as Aliena, a shepherdess. In the forest, they meet a shepherd called Silvius and the girl he loves, called Phoebe.

When Duke Frederick realizes his daughter Celia has run away, he sends Oliver to the forest to look for her. Meanwhile, Orlando and his servant Adam find Duke Senior and his followers living wild in the woodland. Orlando decides to join them in their simple, but happy, way of life.

FIND THESE CHARACTERS ON THE NEXT TWO PAGES

Charles

Silvius

Duke Senior & Followers

Rosalind as Ganymede

Orlando

Oliver

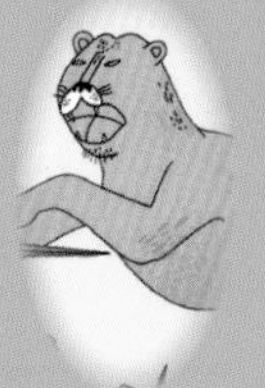
Lioness

Touchstone

Rosalind (still disguised as Ganymede) finds Orlando in the forest, pinning love poems for her on the trees. "Ganymede" offers to meet him every day and teach him how to get over his broken heart. Meanwhile, Phoebe falls in love with "Ganymede," thinking that Rosalind is really a boy.

One day, Oliver appears and explains that Orlando has just saved him from a lioness. He says he is now feeling ashamed of how badly he has treated his brother. Oliver falls in love with Celia (still disguised as Aliena). Rosalind tells everyone to meet the next day, when they will all be married.

The next day, they all meet up with Duke Senior and his men. Rosalind and Celia reveal who they really are, so that they can marry Orlando and Oliver. Now that "Ganymede" has turned out to be a girl, Phoebe agrees to marry Silvius, while Duke Frederick's jester Touchstone marries a local girl, Audrey. During the wedding party, news arrives that Duke Frederick has given up the dukedom and Duke Senior can rightfully claim it back.

# JULIUS CAESAR

### *Setting: Ancient Rome*

*Julius Caesar* is a tragedy and a historical drama, based around real events in ancient Rome. Caesar is a famous general, who is also popular with ordinary Romans. As he grows more and more popular, other important people decide that he must be killed before he becomes too powerful. Sadly, one of the men who wants to kill him is his good friend Brutus. This action-packed play has omens, a ghost, a murder, and a lot of fighting.

Julius Caesar, a great Roman general, returns in triumph from battle. The people of Rome adore him, and cheer him on as he parades down the streets. A fortune-teller, however, warns him to "Beware the ides of March," which means March 15th, but Caesar chooses to ignore him.

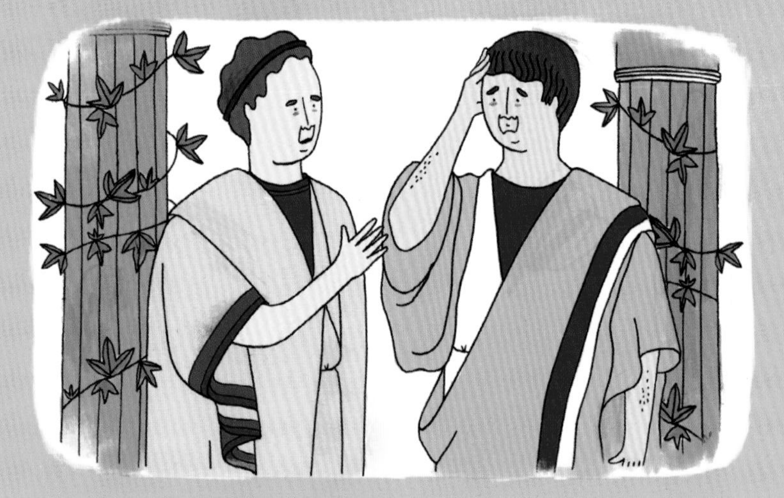

Caesar's friends Brutus and Cassius discuss how popular and powerful he is. They worry that he wants to rule Rome as a king, replacing the system in which a group of men, called the Senate, rule together. Cassius believes Caesar is a bad leader and should not be king. Meanwhile, Caesar tells his friend Mark Antony that he does not trust Cassius.

Another Roman, Casca, tells Brutus and Cassius that Caesar has refused to be king, but Cassius hatches a plot to get rid of Caesar anyway. To get Brutus to join the plot, Cassius sends him fake letters that look like they are from the people of Rome, complaining that Caesar has too much power.

In a meeting at Brutus's house, the plotters agree to kill Caesar, but to spare Mark Antony. Brutus's wife, Portia, asks him what is going on, but he won't tell her. On March 15th, as Caesar sets off for the Senate, his wife, Calpurnia, says she has had bad dreams about it. She begs him not to go—but he does.

FIND THESE CHARACTERS ON THE NEXT TWO PAGES

Cassius Calpurnia

Caesar

Mark Antony

Octavius

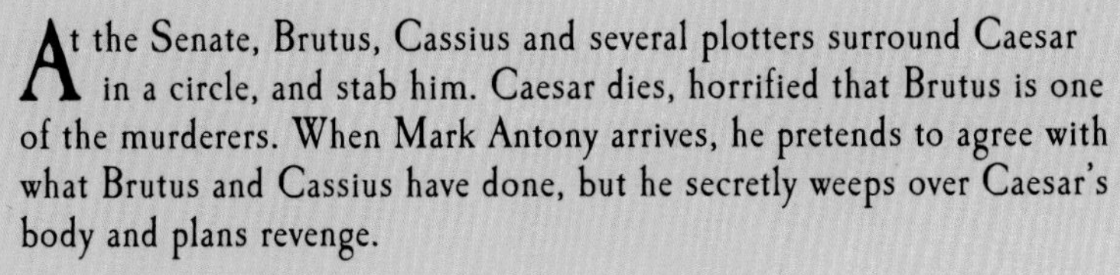

At the Senate, Brutus, Cassius and several plotters surround Caesar in a circle, and stab him. Caesar dies, horrified that Brutus is one of the murderers. When Mark Antony arrives, he pretends to agree with what Brutus and Cassius have done, but he secretly weeps over Caesar's body and plans revenge.

Mark Antony makes a speech to the Roman public that attacks Brutus, and shows the crowd Caesar's body. When the Roman citizens find out that Caesar has left his wealth to them, they angrily turn on Brutus and Cassius and drive them out of the city.

Camped outside Rome with their armies, Brutus and Cassius prepare to fight Mark Antony and his supporters Octavius and Lepidus for control of the city. The night before the battle, Brutus sees Caesar's ghost and is haunted by guilt. The following day, the fighting goes wrong for Brutus and Cassius, and they both kill themselves before they can be captured.

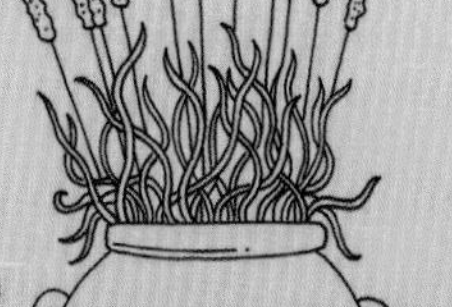

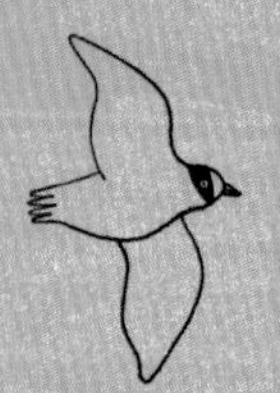

# TWELFTH NIGHT

*Setting: The Kingdom of Illyria*

*Twelfth Night* is a comedy, and once again Shakespeare's plot involves the mix-ups caused by people wearing disguises. When a beautiful lady named Viola dresses up as a man, a countess called Olivia falls in love with her. To add to the confusion, Viola has a twin brother, who she thinks has died in a shipwreck, but he is still alive. Many love letters and secret messages are sent in the play, which create even more madness. However, by the end of the play, all the secrets are revealed and two couples marry.

Orsino, Duke of Illyria, is in love with the beautiful Lady Olivia—but she is in mourning after her brother's death and is not interested in him. While Orsino pines away in his palace, a ship is wrecked in a big storm on the coast nearby.

A young lady named Viola survives the shipwreck, but she cannot find her twin brother, Sebastian, and thinks he is dead. When Viola hears about Duke Orsino she disguises herself as a boy named Cesario, and she goes to work as a page boy at his palace.

As "Cesario," Viola soon becomes Orsino's favorite page boy and she secretly falls in love with him. However, Orsino remains in love with Olivia and sends Viola (still disguised as Cesario) to take his love letters to Olivia's house. When Olivia meets "Cesario," she falls in love with him instead of Orsino.

At Olivia's house, her lazy uncle Sir Toby Belch and his friend Sir Andrew Aguecheek—along with her clown Feste and lady-in-waiting Maria—tease the pompous butler Malvolio. Knowing him to be in love with Olivia, they fake love letters from her, telling him to wear his yellow stockings as a secret sign of love.

FIND THESE CHARACTERS ON THE NEXT TWO PAGES

Orsino

Viola as Cesario

Malvolio

Sir Toby, Sir Andrew, & Maria

Olivia

Antonio

Priest

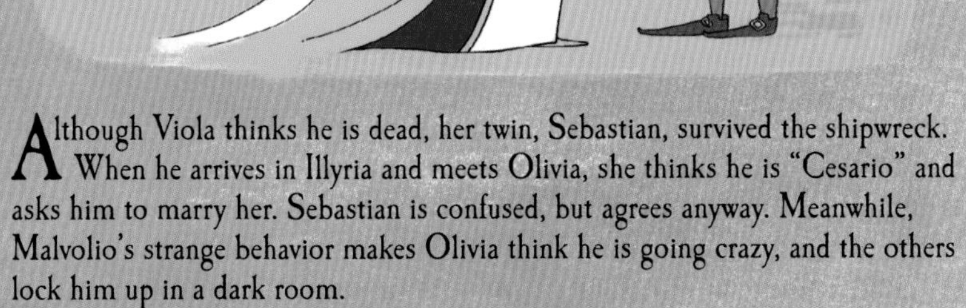

Although Viola thinks he is dead, her twin, Sebastian, survived the shipwreck. When he arrives in Illyria and meets Olivia, she thinks he is "Cesario" and asks him to marry her. Sebastian is confused, but agrees anyway. Meanwhile, Malvolio's strange behavior makes Olivia think he is going crazy, and the others lock him up in a dark room.

Antonio, a sailor who rescued Sebastian from the sea, is arrested for an old crime. When he sees "Cesario," he thinks he is Sebastian and begs him to give back a bag of money he lent him. Still disguised as Cesario, Viola says she doesn't know Antonio, but she realizes that Sebastian must have survived the shipwreck.

Finally, everyone meets up at Olivia's house and the mix-ups get sorted out. Sebastian and Viola are reunited, and Viola reveals that she is really a woman. Malvolio is released, and Orsino realizes he loves Viola, not Olivia. He marries her and then Olivia ends up with Sebastian, meaning everyone (except Malvolio) is happy.

# MACBETH

## *Setting: Medieval Scotland*

*Macbeth* is one of Shakespeare's tragedies. It is about a brave general called Macbeth, who is told by three witches that one day he will become King of Scotland. He tells his wife, who persuades him to murder the king, which he does. However, Macbeth, now king, feels really guilty. Soon, he is haunted by the bad things he has done to win power, and he faces a terrible downfall. Action-packed and supernatural, this is a really spooky play!

After winning a battle for King Duncan of Scotland, Macbeth and his friend Banquo meet three witches on a moor. The witches make three prophecies. They say that Macbeth will become Thane (Lord) of Cawdor, that he will become king, and Banquo's sons will be kings, too.

When King Duncan makes Macbeth the Thane of Cawdor, Macbeth wonders if the prophecy about him becoming king might also come true. Macbeth's wife, Lady Macbeth, would love him to be king. So when Duncan visits, she tells Macbeth to kill him. That night, urged on by his wife, Macbeth stabs Duncan to death in his sleep.

When the murder is discovered, Duncan's sons Malcolm and Donalbain are afraid they'll be blamed, so they run away. Since Macbeth is King Duncan's cousin, he is the next in line to the throne, so he is crowned king.

However, Macbeth suspects Banquo knows the truth. He arranges to have both Banquo and his son Fleance murdered, but Fleance escapes alive. That evening Macbeth sees Banquo's ghost, and is filled with guilt. Lady Macbeth starts seeing things, too, believing she has blood on her hands that will not wash off.

FIND THESE CHARACTERS ON THE NEXT TWO PAGES

Three Witches

Duncan

Macbeth

Banquo's Ghost

Lady Macbeth

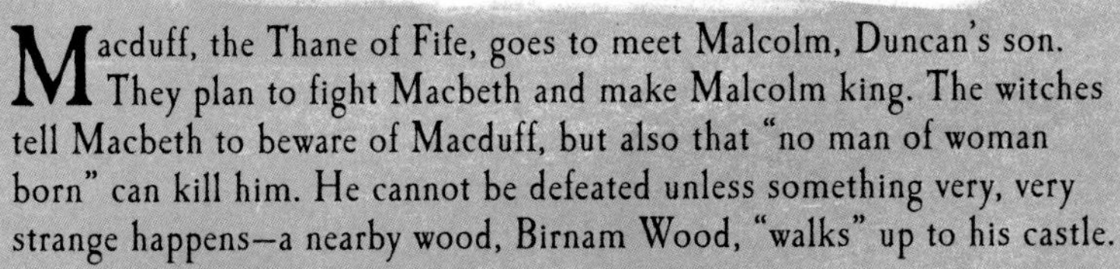

Macduff, the Thane of Fife, goes to meet Malcolm, Duncan's son. They plan to fight Macbeth and make Malcolm king. The witches tell Macbeth to beware of Macduff, but also that "no man of woman born" can kill him. He cannot be defeated unless something very, very strange happens—a nearby wood, Birnam Wood, "walks" up to his castle.

Macbeth cannot find Macduff, but orders his wife and children to be killed instead. When Macduff hears the terrible news, he vows to take revenge. Meanwhile, Lady Macbeth, who has been ill for some time, turns mad and kills herself.

Malcolm and Macduff's armies march to Birnam Wood. They use branches from the trees to camouflage themselves, then walk uphill to attack Macbeth's castle. Macbeth faces Macduff, and tells him "no man of woman born" can harm him. Macduff replies he was not born, but cut out of his mother's body. After a furious sword fight, he slices off Macbeth's head and declares Malcolm king.

# THE TEMPEST

## *Setting: A magical faraway island*

Shakespeare wrote many plays set in castles, cities, and forests, but only *The Tempest* is about an enchanted island. The play begins with a terrible storm, a tempest, created by the magic of a great wizard called Prospero. He wants to shipwreck all his enemies on the island, where he lives with his daughter, Miranda. Prospero then has to use all his magic powers to make sure there's a happy ending.

A terrible storm (or tempest) sinks a ship carrying King Alonso of Naples home from his daughter's wedding. Also on board are Alonso's son Ferdinand, his courtier Gonzalo, his brother Sebastian, and Sebastian's friend Antonio, Duke of Milan. The ship is wrecked on a remote island on which Prospero, a magician, and his daughter Miranda live. They were washed up there years earlier, after Antonio, who is Prospero's brother, threw them out of Milan and stole Prospero's dukedom, with Alonso's help.

Prospero asks Ariel, a flying magical spirit who serves him, to help with his plans for revenge. Ariel finds Ferdinand, Alonso's son, and brings him to meet Miranda. They fall in love at once. Prospero sets Ferdinand to work carrying logs to prove his devotion.

Meanwhile, Alonso, Gonzalo, Sebastian, and Antonio are on another part of the island. Alonso is sad because he is sure his son is dead. While he and Gonzalo sleep, Sebastian and Antonio plot to kill them and take the throne, but Ariel stops them.

FIND THESE CHARACTERS ON THE NEXT TWO PAGES

Miranda

Prospero

Ferdinand

Sebastian & Antonio

Stephano

Trinculo

Ariel

A flamingo

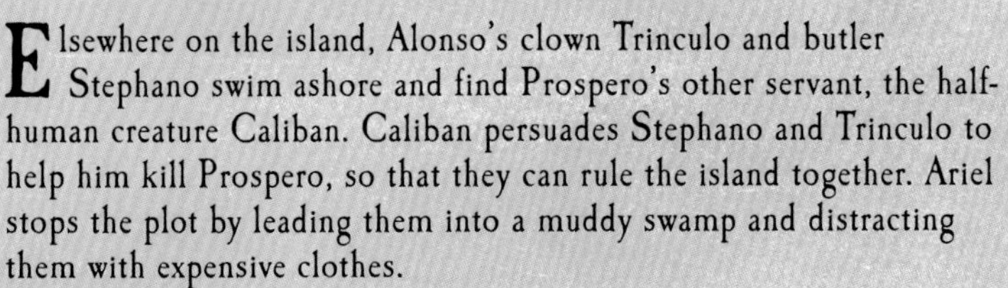

Elsewhere on the island, Alonso's clown Trinculo and butler Stephano swim ashore and find Prospero's other servant, the half-human creature Caliban. Caliban persuades Stephano and Trinculo to help him kill Prospero, so that they can rule the island together. Ariel stops the plot by leading them into a muddy swamp and distracting them with expensive clothes.

Prospero conjures up a magical banquet to tempt Alonso and his followers. However, Ariel appears as a terrifying demon and makes the banquet vanish. Ariel warns them that Prospero knows about their crimes and that Alonso has lost his son Ferdinand as punishment. Alonso feels guilty and is full of remorse.

Finally, Prospero summons everyone to see him and forgives them, saying he will leave the island and his magic behind, and return to Milan as the rightful Duke. He reveals that Ferdinand is alive and will marry his daughter Miranda and sets his servants Ariel and Caliban free. The ship is magically repaired, the crew is safe, and the sea is calm. They all plan to stay on the island for one night, then sail home the next day.

# MUCH ADO ABOUT NOTHING

*Setting: Messina, a city in Sicily*

In this much-loved comedy, Shakespeare tells the story of two couples and the obstacles that stand in the way of their true love. The play is full of jokey conversations and smart tricks that people play on each other—some funny, and some not so funny. Luckily, all the tricks are sorted out, and the story ends happily with a group of weddings.

Don Pedro and his soldiers, including the witty Benedick and the young, handsome Claudio, return from a successful battle to stay at the house of Don Pedro's friend Leonato, the governor of Messina. Leonato lives with his daughter Hero and sharp-tongued niece Beatrice. At a party to celebrate the soldiers' return, Claudio falls in love with Hero, and Don Pedro helps him to woo her. Beatrice and Benedick, however, tease each other rudely, both declaring they will never marry.

Don John, Don Pedro's brother, is jealous of Claudio for being Don Pedro's favorite. He decides to ruin Claudio's happiness with the help of his servant Borachio. They arrange for Borachio to visit his girlfriend, Margaret, Hero's lady-in-waiting, but to make it look as if it is Hero he is visiting.

Meanwhile, Beatrice and Benedick's friends, who can see they are made for each other, hatch a plot to trick them. They make sure that Beatrice overhears them saying that Benedick is deeply in love with her. Then they play the same trick on Benedick. It works and they both fall in love, but they do not tell each other!

FIND THESE CHARACTERS ON THE NEXT TWO PAGES

Don Pedro

Leonato

Don John

Benedick

Dogberry

Verges

Hero

The night before Claudio's wedding, Don John tricks him and Don Pedro into thinking that Borachio has been wooing "Hero" at her window, though in reality it is Margaret at the window. Thinking Hero has betrayed him, Claudio angrily refuses to marry her the next day. Shocked and upset, Hero faints and appears to be dead. Benedick and Beatrice discuss what has happened and admit that they love each other.

Hero recovers and her family decide to hide her away to make Claudio feel guilty, but Don Pedro and Claudio don't know this and think she has died. The police chief Dogberry and his assistant Verges discover Borachio's crime, and Don John's evil plot is revealed. However, Don John manages to escape.

Claudio feels really guilty, so he agrees to marry Hero's cousin, whom he has never met. As he waits at the altar, his bride approaches in a veil, then lifts it to reveal she is the real Hero, who has been alive all along. The happy couple are married and Benedick asks Beatrice to marry him, too. At first they argue, but Benedick finally kisses Beatrice and they agree to get married.

# ANTONY & CLEOPATRA

## *Setting: Ancient Egypt and the Roman Empire*

*Antony and Cleopatra* is a play about power, politics, and passionate love. Antony, one of the rulers of ancient Rome, abandons his responsibilities, friends, and home in Rome to be with Queen Cleopatra of Egypt. Not surprisingly, things start to go from bad to worse. However, even faced with disaster, Antony cannot live without his love ... The play ends with one of Shakespeare's great death scenes, featuring a basket of poisonous snakes.

Antony is one of the three rulers of ancient Rome, but he spends most of his time in Egypt, where he has fallen in love with the glamorous queen, Cleopatra. Rome's other two rulers, Octavius Caesar and Lepidus, discuss Antony and his selfish behavior.

In Egypt, news arrives from Rome that Antony's wife, Fulvia, has died and that Pompey, a popular young soldier, is planning to gather an army to fight the three rulers for power. Antony decides to return to Rome to face up to his responsibilities.

When he arrives in Rome, Antony agrees to marry Octavius Caesar's sister Octavia to repair his relationship with Caesar. Antony's friend Enobarbus says Antony still loves Cleopatra and will return to her. When Cleopatra hears about the marriage, she is mad with jealousy.

In Rome, Antony, Lepidus, Octavius Caesar, and Pompey agree to make peace and celebrate by drinking together. One of Pompey's men suggests a plot to kill the three rulers and grab power, but Pompey refuses to behave in a dishonorable way.

FIND THESE CHARACTERS ON THE NEXT TWO PAGES

Lepidus

Antony

Octavius

Octavia

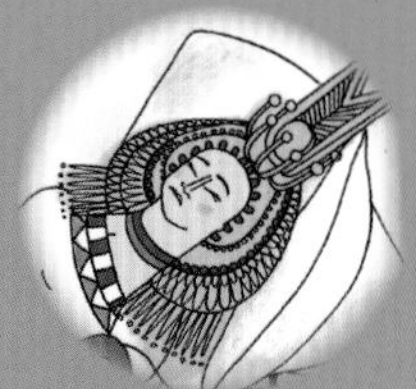
Cleopatra

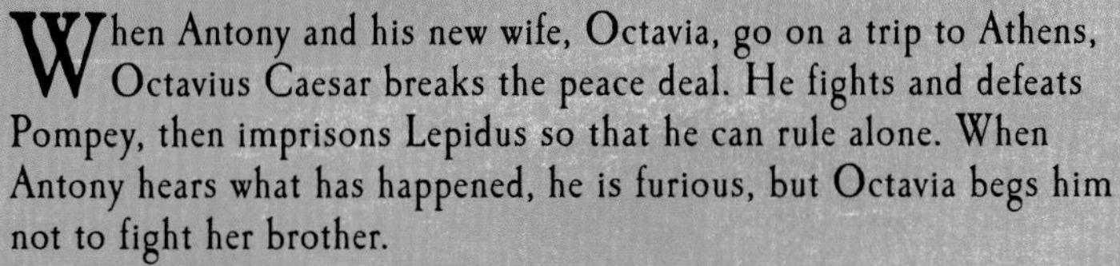

When Antony and his new wife, Octavia, go on a trip to Athens, Octavius Caesar breaks the peace deal. He fights and defeats Pompey, then imprisons Lepidus so that he can rule alone. When Antony hears what has happened, he is furious, but Octavia begs him not to fight her brother.

Antony sends Octavia back to Rome and returns to Egypt. With Cleopatra's help, he gathers an army to fight Octavius Caesar. However, Octavius sends his troops to Egypt and defeats Antony and Cleopatra in a series of battles. Antony blames Cleopatra for the defeat and they have a terrible argument.

Enobarbus, disgusted with Antony's behavior, leaves him and joins Octavius, but then dies of sadness. Cleopatra hides from Antony and sends him a message saying she has died. Antony is so upset he tries to kill himself by falling onto his own sword. He is taken to Cleopatra and they forgive each other before Antony dies. Octavius captures Cleopatra, but she has arranged for a basket of deadly snakes to be delivered in secret. She and her loyal lady-in-waiting Charmian let the snakes bite them, preferring to die rather than to be held captive.

# A MIDSUMMER NIGHT'S DREAM

*Setting: A forest outside ancient Athens*

This play is a comedy, set in an enchanted forest in ancient Greece. There are three separate stories that all connect—it can seem a little complicated! A celebration is taking place because the Duke of Athens is marrying Queen Hippolyta, and all the action takes place around this event. There are plenty of fabulous and funny characters, including a fairy king and queen, a mischievous fairy called Puck, four young lovers, and a group of clueless actors.

Egeus wants his daughter Hermia to marry Demetrius, but she prefers Lysander. Duke Theseus tells Hermia to obey her father or become a nun. She must make her choice before the Duke marries Queen Hippolyta in a few days' time.

Hermia and Lysander run away to the forest. Demetrius's ex-girlfriend, Helena, who still loves him, tells Demetrius their secret. He goes to find Hermia, with Helena following. Meanwhile, a group of workmen rehearse a play in the forest for the wedding.

In the forest, Oberon, the fairy king, decides to trick his wife, Titania, by putting a magic potion on her eyes while she sleeps. The potion will make her fall in love with the first thing she sees when she wakes up. Oberon also sees that Demetrius is rejecting Helena's love. So, he tells his servant Puck to find Demetrius and put the potion on the man's eyes. Oberon believes that when Demetrius wakes up and sees Helena, he will fall in love with her again, which will make Helena happy.

FIND THESE CHARACTERS ON THE NEXT TWO PAGES

Theseus

Lysander & Hermia

Oberon & Titania

Puck

Bottom

The Actors

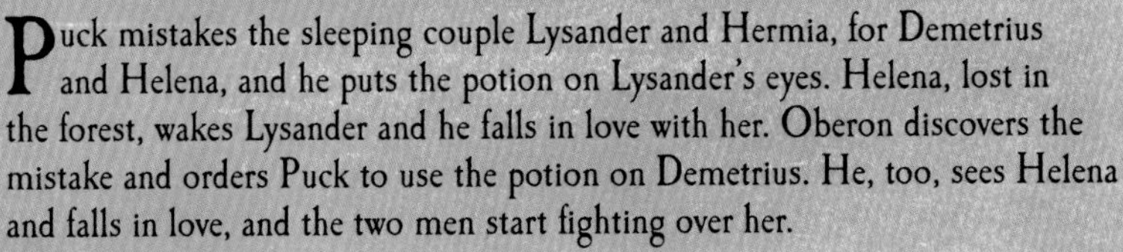
Puck mistakes the sleeping couple Lysander and Hermia, for Demetrius and Helena, and he puts the potion on Lysander's eyes. Helena, lost in the forest, wakes Lysander and he falls in love with her. Oberon discovers the mistake and orders Puck to use the potion on Demetrius. He, too, sees Helena and falls in love, and the two men start fighting over her.

Meanwhile, as a group of workmen rehearse their play, the mischievous Puck plays a trick on the star actor, Bottom, turning his head into that of a donkey. His fellow actors run away in fright, leaving Bottom alone with the fairy queen, Titania. When she wakes up, the first thing she sees is Bottom, and the magic potion makes her fall in love with him.

Finally, Oberon frees Titania and Lysander from the spell, so Lysander is free again to love Hermia, but Demetrius stays in love with Helena. When Theseus sees this, he ignores Egeus's wishes and declares a joint wedding. After the wedding feast, the workmen perform their play. Although it's supposed to be a tragedy, their bumbling performance is really funny. Puck asks the audience to remember the play as if it had been a dream.

# ROMEO & JULIET

*Setting: Verona, Italy*

*Romeo and Juliet* is one of the most famous love stories ever written. Set in Verona in Italy, it's about a boy and girl who fall in love but whose families are bitter enemies. Romeo and Juliet are so in love that they ignore their families' bitter quarrels and marry in secret. It seems like the play should have a happy ending but, sadly, it doesn't. Instead, it ends with one of Shakespeare's most heartbreaking death scenes.

In the city of Verona, two wealthy families, the Montagues and the Capulets, have been arguing for years. A fight breaks out between servants from the two houses and other members of the families get involved, too. Prince Escalus, the ruler of Verona, orders that any further fighting will be punishable by death.

Romeo Montague's parents tell Benvolio, their nephew, that Romeo seems unhappy. Romeo confesses to Benvolio that he loves a girl named Rosaline. Hearing that she will be at a party at the Capulets' house that night, they decide to sneak in, wearing masks as a disguise.

At the Capulets' house, Juliet Capulet's mother tells her that Count Paris, who hopes to marry her, will be coming to the party. Juliet is shocked, because she is only 13 years old. As the party begins, Romeo, Benvolio, and their friend Mercutio sneak in. Juliet's cousin Tybalt Capulet recognizes them, but Juliet's father, Old Capulet, stops him from killing his Montague enemy. Meanwhile, Romeo sees Juliet dancing with Count Paris and instantly falls head over heels in love with her.

FIND THESE CHARACTERS ON THE NEXT TWO PAGES

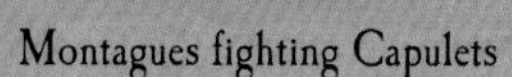
Montagues fighting Capulets

Rosaline

Benvolio & Mercutio

Juliet

Friar Laurence

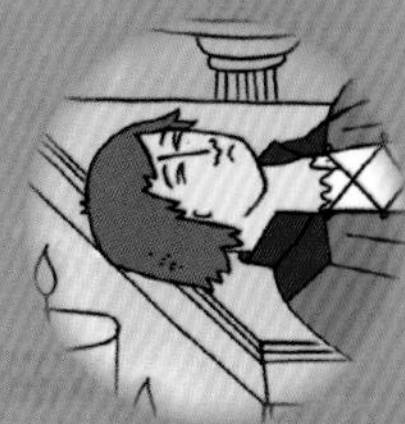
Romeo

Romeo follows Juliet and kisses her, but her nurse separates them. After the party, Romeo climbs into the Capulets' yard and sees Juliet on her balcony. Although their families are enemies, the two of them declare their love for each other and agree to marry the following day.

With the help of Juliet's nurse and the monk Friar Laurence, Romeo and Juliet secretly marry. However, later that day, in the town square, Tybalt confronts Romeo and his friends for sneaking into the party. A fight breaks out; Tybalt kills Mercutio, and Romeo kills Tybalt. Because Romeo was provoked, he is not sentenced to death, but he is told he has to leave Verona forever.

Friar Laurence and the nurse arrange for Romeo to spend one night with Juliet before leaving for nearby Mantua. However, Old Capulet arranges for Juliet to marry Count Paris. Juliet is horrified and begs the friar for help. He gives her a potion that will make her seem dead for 48 hours, so the wedding will be called off and she can escape to Mantua.

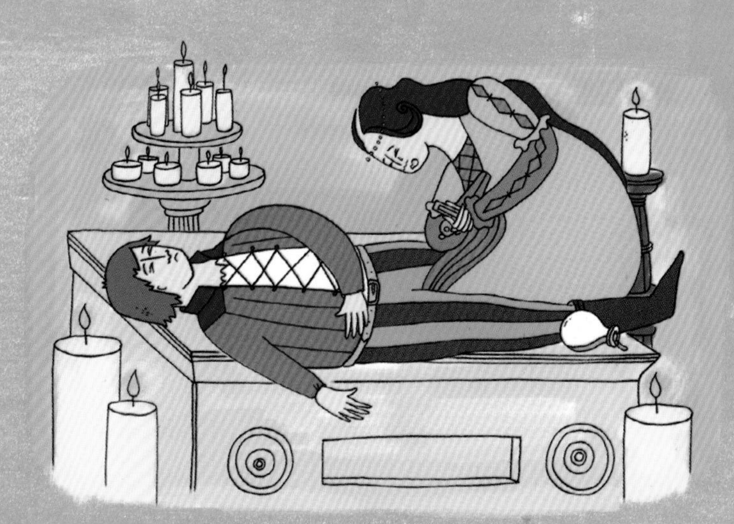

Juliet takes the potion while Friar Laurence sends a message to Romeo to explain the plan. However, the message doesn't arrive, and instead Romeo hears news that Juliet has died. He buys poison and returns to Verona. In the Capulet vault, he finds Count Paris visiting Juliet's body. He kills Paris in a fight, takes the poison and dies. When Juliet wakes up and sees what has happened, she kills herself with Romeo's dagger.

# HAMLET

## *Setting: Elsinore, Denmark*

Set in Denmark, *Hamlet* is one of Shakespeare's greatest and most powerful plays. At the beginning of the play, Hamlet is visited by his father's ghost, who tells him that he was murdered by his own brother Claudius, who has now replaced him as king. Hamlet vows to seek revenge on his uncle, and what follows is a story of anger, madness, and tragedy which, by the end, leaves only one character alive to tell Hamlet's tale. Read on to see who it is.

Hamlet, Prince of Denmark, hears from the castle guards and his friend Horatio that they have seen a ghost on the castle battlements. It is the ghost of Hamlet's father, who has recently died and been replaced as king by his brother Claudius. The ghost tells Hamlet that Claudius murdered him by pouring poison in his ear, and that Hamlet must take revenge.

Claudius has also married Gertrude, Hamlet's mother. He orders Hamlet to stay at home instead of returning to his college studies. Hamlet hates Claudius and wants revenge, but first he needs to be sure that Claudius is really guilty of killing his father. He decides to pretend to be mad while he thinks about what to do.

Hamlet's strange behavior upsets his girlfriend, Ophelia, the daughter of the royal adviser Polonius. Claudius and Gertrude send two of Hamlet's friends, Rosencrantz and Guildenstern, to spy on him. Claudius spies on Hamlet, too, but no one can work out what is wrong with him.

When a group of actors visits the castle, Hamlet arranges for them to perform a play about a king being murdered by his brother by pouring poison in his ear to see if it upsets Claudius. It does, but when Hamlet finds Claudius praying, he doesn't kill him, because being killed while praying might send Claudius to heaven.

FIND THESE CHARACTERS ON THE NEXT TWO PAGES

King Hamlet's Ghost · Guards · Rosencrantz & Guildenstern · Claudius · Polonius · Ophelia · Hamlet · Laertes · Gertrude

Hamlet goes to his mother Gertrude's room. He sees that someone is hiding behind a curtain and thinks it is Claudius, so he stabs and kills him; however, it turns out it was Ophelia's father, Polonius. To get rid of Hamlet, Claudius sends him to England with Rosencrantz and Guildenstern, with instructions to the English king to have him killed. But Hamlet escapes and heads back to Denmark.

Because she lost her father, Ophelia turns mad from the grief and drowns. Her brother Laertes is furious with Hamlet over the deaths of his father and sister. Claudius and Laertes plan for Laertes to fight Hamlet in a duel, secretly using a poisoned blade so that he will kill Hamlet.

Hamlet arrives back in Denmark to find Ophelia being buried and Laertes ready to fight. The duel begins and Hamlet does well, so Claudius offers him a poisoned drink. He refuses it, but Gertrude drinks some and dies. Hamlet's and Laertes' swords get mixed up and they are both scratched by the poisoned blade. Before dying, Laertes tells Hamlet what Claudius has done. Hamlet stabs Claudius to death before dying himself. Only Hamlet's old friend Horatio is left to tell the story.

# ANSWERS

*As You Like It, 6–7*

*Julius Caesar, 10–11*

*Twelfth Night, 14–15*

*Macbeth, 18–19*

*The Tempest, 22–23*

*Much Ado About Nothing, 26–27*

## *Antony & Cleopatra, 30–31*

## *A Midsummer Night's Dream, 34–35*

*Romeo & Juliet, 38–39*

*Hamlet, 42–43*

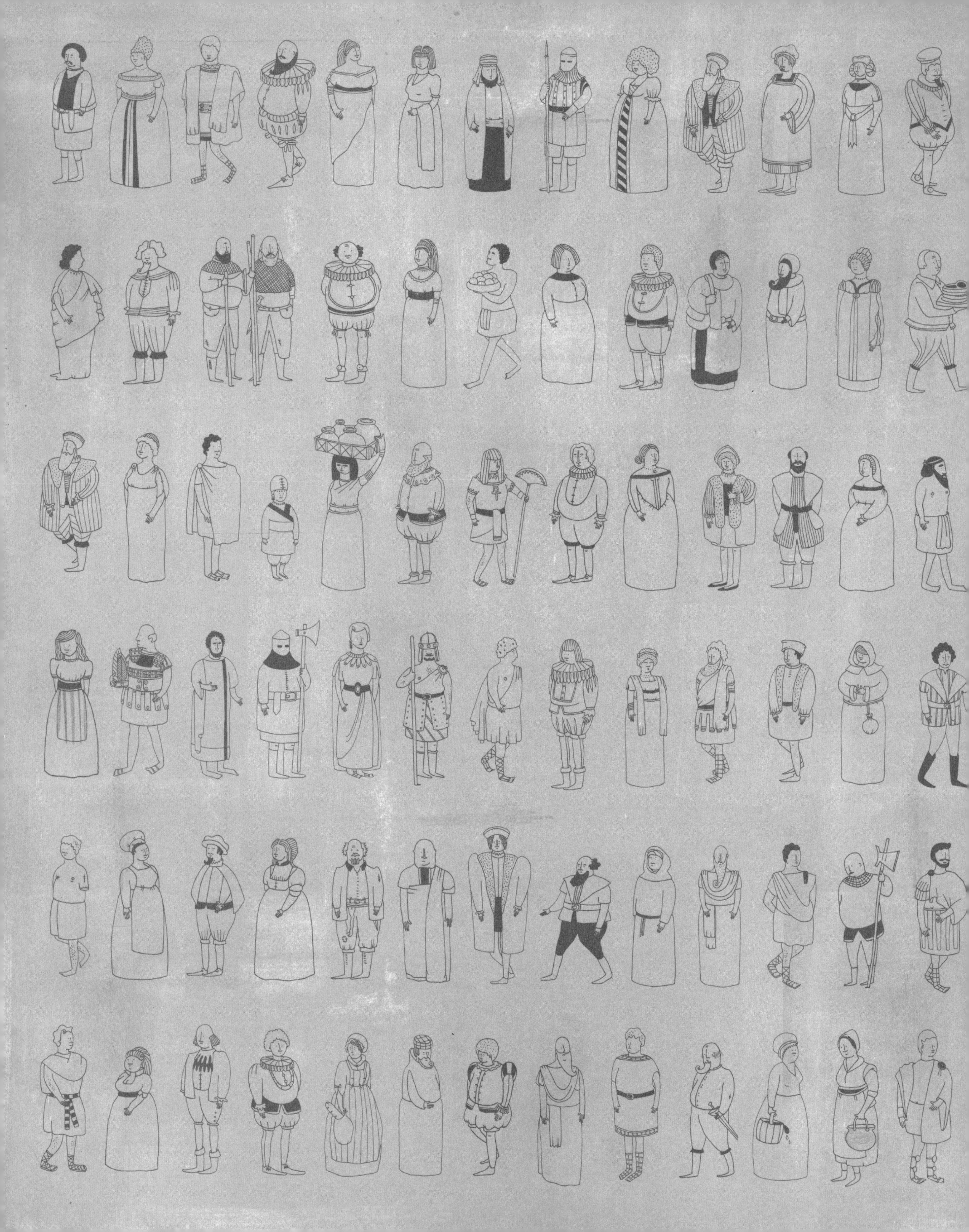